My Path to Math

1 2 3 4 5 6 7 8 9

ROMAN NUMERALS AND ORDINALS

Kylie Burns

Crabtree Publishing Company

www.crabtreebooks.com

Author: Kylie Burns
Publishing plan research and development:
  Sean Charlebois, Reagan Miller
  Crabtree Publishing Company
Editor: Molly Aloian
Editorial director: Kathy Middleton
Project coordinator: Margaret Salter
Prepress technician: Margaret Salter
Coordinating editor: Chester Fisher
Series editor: Jessica Cohn
Project manager: Kumar Kunal (Q2AMEDIA)
Art direction: Cheena Yadav (Q2AMEDIA)
Cover design: Shruti Aggarwal (Q2AMEDIA)
Design: Shruti Aggarwal (Q2AMEDIA)
Photo research: Iti Shrotriya (Q2AMEDIA)

Photographs:
Corbis: Craig Hutchins: title page
Dreamstime: Andrew Kazmierski: front cover; Alena Katanaeva: p. 5 (top);
  Jacek Chabraszewski: p. 5; Dragan Trifunovic: p. 13; Akhilesh Sharma:
  p. 21 (bottom), p. 23
Istockphoto: Reuben Schultz: front cover; Anthony Berenyi: p. 9 (bottom);
  Stacie Andrea: p. 21 (middle)
Photolibrary: The Print Collector: p. 15; Guy Bouchet-Cardinale/
  Photononstop: p. 20; Robert Lawson: p. 21 (top);
Shutterstock: Alhovik: front cover; Marsha Goldenberg: p. 5 (inset); Drfelice:
  p. 6; Robert Forrest: p. 7; Syoma: p. 4, p. 9 (top); Vita Khorzhevska: p. 11;
  Michael Levy: p. 16-17

Q2AMedia Art Bank: p. 12, p. 13, p. 14, p. 19

Library and Archives Canada Cataloguing in Publication

Burns, Kylie
    Roman numerals and ordinals / Kylie Burns.

(My path to math)
Includes index.
ISBN 978-0-7787-5250-9 (bound).--ISBN 978-0-7787-5297-4 (pbk.)

    1. Roman numerals--Juvenile literature. 2. Numbers, Ordinal--Juvenile
literature. I. Title. II. Series: My path to math

QA141.3.B87 2009   j513.5   C2009-905360-8

Library of Congress Cataloging-in-Publication Data

Burns, Kylie.
  Roman numerals and ordinals / Kylie Burns.
    p. cm. -- (My path to math)
  Includes index.
  ISBN 978-0-7787-5250-9 (reinforced lib. bdg. : alk. paper) -- ISBN 978-0-7787-
5297-4 (pbk. : alk. paper)
  1. Roman numerals--Juvenile literature. 2. Numbers, Ordinal--Juvenile
literature. I. Title. II. Series.

  QA41.B97 2010
  513.5--dc22

                                        2009035493

Crabtree Publishing Company

www.crabtreebooks.com   1-800-387-7650

Printed in China/122009/CT20090903

Published in Canada
Crabtree Publishing
616 Welland Ave.
St. Catharines, ON
L2M 5V6

Published in the United States
Crabtree Publishing
PMB 59051
350 Fifth Avenue, 59th Floor
New York, New York 10118

Published in the United Kingdom
Crabtree Publishing
Maritime House
Basin Road North, Hove
BN41 1WR

Published in Australia
Crabtree Publishing
386 Mt. Alexander Rd.
Ascot Vale (Melbourne)
VIC 3032

XI

Contents

XI

Time for Fun!

Abby and Ben are going to the amusement park with their mom and dad. Abby wants to try the roller coaster. Ben wants to go to the magic show.

"How much time do we have?" asks Ben. He looks at the big clock over the ticket booth. But the clock has letters, not numbers! Dad explains that the letters are called **Roman numerals**.

In Roman numerals, ▶ letters stand for numbers.

Activity Box

Look at the clock. Which Roman numeral is in the place of the number 5? Which is in the place of the 10?

Numerals and Numbers

Roman numerals are a number system from long ago. This system uses seven letters: I, V, X, L, C, D, and M. The letters stand alone or side by side to show different values.

We use **digits** in our number system. We use ten digits: 1, 2, 3, 4, 5, 6, 7, 8, 9, and 0. The digits stand alone or side by side to show different values, too.

Activity Box

Which of the seven letters used for Roman numerals is closest to your age?

▼ There is no **symbol** for zero in Roman numerals!

ROMAN NUMERALS

I = 1

V = 5

X = 10

L = 50

C = 100

D = 500

M = 1,000

XI

What Time Is It?

Ben wants to know the time, but he cannot read the Roman numerals on the clock. Dad gives Ben a hint. He shows Ben his watch. The watch says that it is ten o'clock.

The Roman numerals on the clock stand for the same numbers on the watch. Ben sees that the numeral X stands for 10.

$$X = 10$$

Activity Box

If it is 10:00 now, what time will it be in an hour? Which Roman numeral will the little hand point to then?

◄ Which Roman numerals
do the hands point to?

A digital watch ▶
uses digits!

XI

Numeral Art

Dad explains that our numbers show **place value**. When we see the number 11, we know that there is 1 ten and 1 one.

Roman numerals do not show place value the same way. We read Roman numerals differently. We read them from left to right. If a Roman numeral repeats itself, we use **addition**! We add the numerals that repeat in order to figure out the number.

I stands for 1.
II stands for 2, because 1+1=2.
III stands for 3, because 1+1+1=3.

Activity Box

When a Roman numeral repeats itself, we use addition. The Roman numeral XX stands for 10+10. Add two 10s to find out what the numeral XX stands for!

Study the clock on page 9. Try writing the Roman numerals for 1 through 12.

XI

Count Back

Ben sees a pattern in the numerals I, II, and III. The I is repeated. He asks why IV is different. To explain, Dad points to the bumper cars. Five cars are lined up at the gate. "We need four cars," he says. "Four is one less than five."

Dad explains that we also use **subtraction** to read Roman numerals. If a smaller numeral is in front of a bigger numeral, we start with the bigger numeral. Then we subtract the smaller numeral from the bigger one. In other words, we count back from the bigger numeral.

I = 1 and V = 5
IV means: 1 less than 5.
So, IV = 4.

I = 1 and X = 10
IX means: 1 less than 10.
So, IX = 9

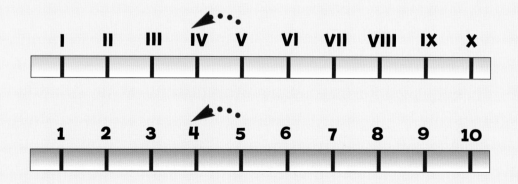

The family needs IV cars. That is one fewer than V.

XI

Counting On

Ben and Abby have fun on the bumpers cars. Then they wait in a line for the water zoom. There are six people ahead of them in the line. In Roman numerals, the number 6 looks like this: VI.

The numeral V is greater than the numeral I. When a bigger numeral is followed by a smaller numeral, we add them together. When we read VI, we can think of this **equation**: 5 + 1 = 6

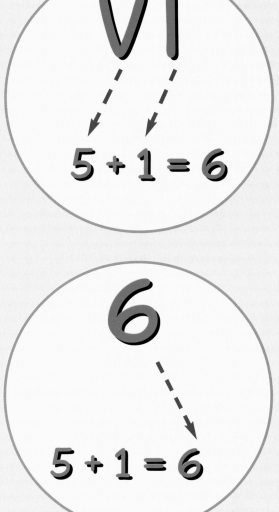

VI

5 + 1 = 6

6

5 + 1 = 6

Activity Box

Write VIII as an equation. Then write XI as an equation.

How many people are shown? What does the Roman numeral look like?

XI

Follow the Order!

The family goes on the rides in a certain order. **Ordinal numbers** help us tell the order of things. Ordinals show the order of things in a **set**. Ordinals can be written as words. Ordinals can also be written as a number followed by two letters.

How many people ▶
are in the sixth car?

second
2nd

first
1st

Activity Box

Which two letters follow the number 19 to show the ordinal number for nineteenth?

Look below at the ordinals written as words. See the **cardinal numbers** and letters that mean the same thing.

first = 1st
second = 2nd
third = 3rd

third
3rd

fourth
4th

fifth
5th

sixth
6th

seventh
7th

XI

What is Next?

The family cannot stay at the park all day. They plan their time carefully. They look at a map and decide where to go. The map helps them figure out the best order to visit the places they want to go.

Mom makes a list of the things they want to do. She writes her list using ordinal numbers.

1st - Bumper Cars
2nd - Water Zoom
3rd - Roller Coaster
4th - Games
5th - Lunch
6th - Magic Show

Activity Box

Look at the map of the park. Now check Mom's list. Where will they go after the water zoom?

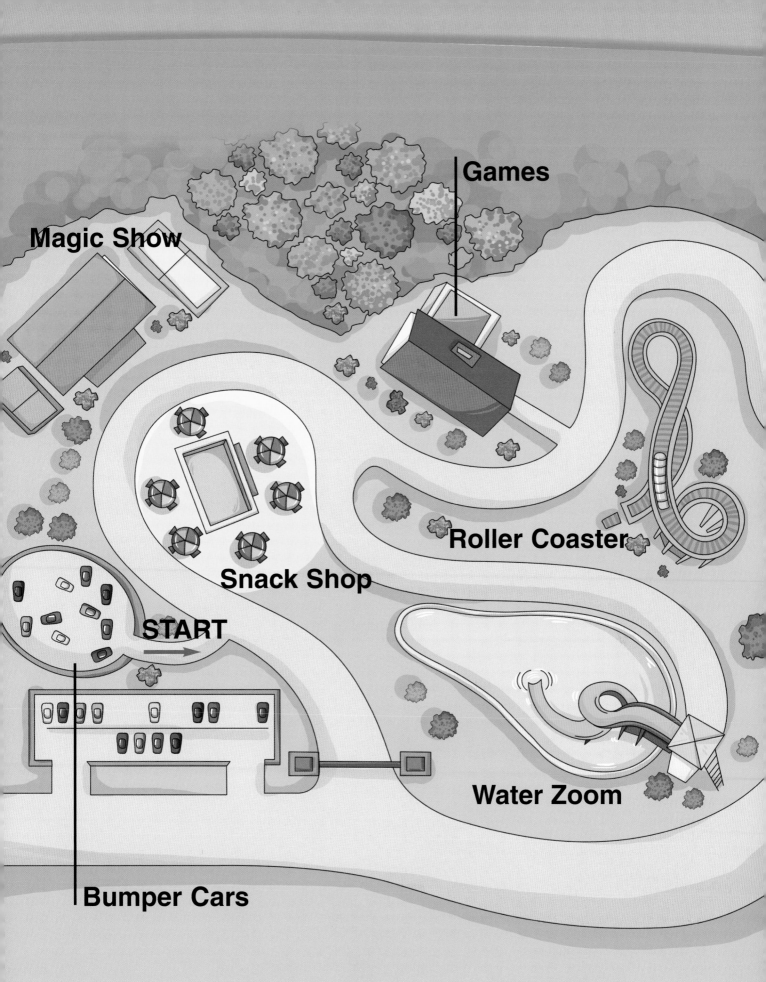

Games

Magic Show

Snack Shop

Roller Coaster

START

Water Zoom

Bumper Cars

19

XI

Put It All Together

Roman numerals and ordinal numbers are found all around the amusement park.

Abby and Ben play the Duck Pond game. Abby wins a stuffed animal on her third try.

Ben wins first prize at the Ring Toss game. His prize is a watch with Roman numerals on it. Mom asks Ben to tell the time with his new watch. It is 12:00. Time for lunch!

◄ Ben is in the second grade. Abby is in the fourth grade. What grade are you in?

BURGER GRILL

1/4 POUNDER BURGER - 1/2 POUNDER BURGER - JUMBO HOT DOGS - CHEESEBURGERS

MENU

HOT & COLD BEVERAGES

◀ They stop at the first burger cart they see.

The first four rings ▶ that Ben tosses miss the bottles. His fifth try is lucky!

◀ At noon, both hands are on XII. You can use the glossary and index that follow to think again about how Roman numerals and ordinals work.

Glossary

addition Combination of two or more amounts to get a bigger amount

cardinal numbers Symbols that show how many items there are in a set, such as 1, or 12, or 25

digits Number symbols

equation A number sentence with an equal sign to show equal amounts

ordinal numbers Cardinal numbers combined with letters to show place or position; or the full words that do the same

place value Worth or measure of a digit, based on its place in a number

Roman numerals System of letter symbols, called numerals, which stand for different amounts

set Items in a collection

subtraction Combination of amounts in which a difference is found, by taking one amount away from another amount

symbol Something that stands for something else

Index